Anxiety & Me

Why doesn't anyone talk about it?
Let's talk about it!

ROBIN COOLEY

Copyright © 2019 by Robin Cooley

All rights reserved. This book or any portion thereof may not be reproduced or used in any manner whatsoever without the express written permission of the publisher except for the use of brief quotations in a book review.

Printed in the United States of America
First Printing, 2019

ISBN: 978-0-578-59021-9

Book design by TeaBerryCreative.com

Acknowledgements

I want to say thank you to my lord first, without him i wouldn't be able to write this book! I also want to say to my husband. Roman, you are a great husband and friend. Thank your for all your love, support and encouragement. You are my rock!!

I want to thank my close friend, Kathi. Thank you for all your support and helping me get through a tough time in my life.

I want to say thank you to the people in my professional life that took the courage to give me their stories. I hope your stories will help others to see their not alone. Thank you!

Contents

Why Doesn't Anyone Want To Talk About It? Let's Talk About It!

I want to say that if your reading this book that you are for sure fed up with your nervous, Anxiety, and severe PANIC ATTACKS. Am I right? I Know you just want some help. Guess what? I am here to help you as best as I can. I want to show you how to manage your anxiety and panic attacks.

I am not a doctor by no means. This is a book on a real person's experience with anxiety and panic attacks. I have been suffering from this awful anxiety roller coaster for some time now. I have met others and talked to them about their experiences which I will share some of them with you, so you can see your not alone in this. Or that you don't feel alone.

I wanted to write a book on the real deal experiences and some great advice on how to help you with the struggle. It will be from a real person not some Medical professional or whoever who has never ever had an anxiety attack or panic attack in their whole life. I have read all the blogs that I could get ahold of and I have read lots of books on this debilitating illness. YES, that's what I call it. Because it sure feels like an illness. Doesn't it?

I am going to talk to you like you are sitting right in front of me and we're having a cup of coffee or a drink. Whichever you prefer. I hope you can believe that I know exactly what you're going through, so there is no secrets here between us. We will have a great conversation. I will do my best to give you some sound good advice that you can use everyday to help you get through the tough times.

Know think that if you read this book. From beginning to end, that it will help you a great deal. It might even cure you. I mean come on! You have to be tired of all the ups and downs of this nervous illness. Aren't you? If you are sick of it then keep on reading. I really don't know how long it viil be till we are fully cured. So, let's get to learning how to deal with this thing on a daily basis. With the positive attitude that it will take to overthrow the illness and lead a healthy, loving, fun life, one that we were meant to have.

I know what you're thinking! How in the world am I supposed to think positive when I am so full of anxiety all the time. Trust me on this, with patience, practice and time and a very positive attitude. You can and you will recover.

I have read and after a time experienced that anxiety comes from fear and your attitude towards that fear. Think about it. It does make some sense. I want you to believe this. If you change your thoughts about this whole situation, it could help you tremendously. I know it will take some time, but it can be done. Maybe your cure will come soon. Just don't give up on yourself.

I hope you stick with this book as I know it can help you. Keep on reading. Get ready for a good change in your life!

My Story!

Why me? I used to ask myself that question all the time when I first started getting these awful panic attacks and of course the dreaded anxiety. So, I am going to tell you how it started with me.

I went to the doctor one day because my right leg was hurting. It had been hurting for a while. Now I know your already thinking! Why is she telling me about her leg. I am getting there.

So, I go in the doctor office. This is a first time for me going to a primary doctor I have always thought I was in good health. I worked out every day. I tried to eat right. Well most of the time. Anyway, I was sitting in the waiting room. Now I don't know about you but I hate going to any doctor I could just feel my heart pounding. I believe that's what they call white coat syndrome. So, I go in the office.

I am sitting there waiting. My husband goes with me as I felt I needed his encouragement for whatever news I was going to get. The doctor comes in and checks my blood pressure first. Of course it was sky high. He freaks out and starts yelling at me. Telling me I had to get on bp meds right away. I told him I was just nervous about going to the doctor He proceeded to tell me there is no such thing as white coat syndrome. I told him he was wrong. This of course set the mood. I have to say I don't ever remember going to a doctor that was so aggressive.

He sent me to get some blood work done, x-ray on my leg. You know all the good ,fun stuff. I remember leaving the doctor and had extreme anxiety. I told my husband I felt shaky. I had no idea this was the beginning of my nightmare with anxiety and panic attacks. I go get all the blood work and x-rays he told me to. I had to wait a week to get my blood work back.

Here I go again. I go in his office, again with my hubby. We are sitting there. The nurse checks my bp and of course its through the roof. I immediately start to panic, because I know what he is going to say. I really didn't expect his response when he came in. I have to say I have never ever met anyone so aggressive speaking and not in a good way in the medical field. He walked in and pulled up his chair way to close to my face and said. "Your blood pressure is in dangerous level and you cholesterol is really high," and "If you don't get on these pills now you will DIE in three to five years." Now I don't have to tell you how that just took the lid of my anxiety.

I sat there and looked at him, then I looked at my husband and his eyes were really wide open and his jaw had dropped. I don't know how I held my panic in so good at the time. OH, by the way I never did get an answer about my leg! I could feel my eyes tear up. This is not what I expected at all. I mean this guy was right in my face yelling. He proceeded to tell me horror stories of people he treated in the past that would not get on their meds or lose weight. How bad it was for them before they died and how short of life they had.

I just sat there and thought what in the world is wrong with this guy. Yes, I had read all the reviews on him before I went to him. I read where he was such a great doctor. He told me to loose some weight and stay on my meds. That this would save my life! I get home and could not. I mean could not shake off this horrible nervous feeling. It scared me so bad. I don't remember anyone scaring me like that. I just kept thinking of how he told me I had three to five years left to live if I didn't take my meds and loose some weight. Now I am not that over weight. I am about 50lbs overweight. I know that's a lot. I do lift weights. So, it cannot be all fat.

I couldn't sleep for two nights. I felt exhausted by the whole experience. I decided to google the meds that I was prescribed. Now I don't suggest that when your nerves are high. I would wait till you have calmed down. I researched them and of course everything on the net either says cancer of your going to die. Now let's not forget the meds side effects. WOW... that alone will scare you. I decided not to take the cholesterol meds as I had read that you can lower your cholesterol naturally. As I found out that is just not true especially if your cholesterol is really high. I am pretty sure I just didn't want to take any meds. I take the bp meds and they were making me feel bad. I didn't take my cholesterol meds. Which in hindsight I should of started them.

I am sitting at home about three days later from seeing the scary doctor I have to tell you I was still in shock about the whole situation. All of a sudden, my heart starts beating really hard, my vision starts gets blurry which made my heart beat faster and faster. My arms start hurting and my hands and feet go numb. It's about one o'clock in the afternoon. I am totally losing it. I call my husband who was working close. He rushed home and in still in his work clothes takes me to the emergency room. Our hospital is about ten minutes from our house so thank God for that. I really thought I was having a heart attack, as I had never had those feelings before. I had seen the commercials and read accidentally before all this happened. I thought I was having the real deal.

I get to the emergency room and tell them I thought I was having a heart attack. Now, I don't know if you know this or not, but if you tell the er that you are having a heart attack they get you right in, no waiting. Unless of course there is someone who is bleeding out. The first thing they did was hook me up to a EKG. My bp was high. The nurses just kept telling me to take deep breaths. That was my first deep breathing exercises. Which by the way is very useful for panic attacks and anxiety as I later learned. I get admitted and am lying there for at least four hours. I took a lot of tests. I took a brain scan and other test to see if I was having a heat attack or maybe a stroke. They did give me a Xanax to calm me down as I was all hyped up.

So get this. The emergency room doctor comes in. He comes in to tell me that all the test look great and I'm ok. I ask him then what the hell is going on with me. The doctor is kind of a comedian, or at least he thinks so! Me, not so much!! The doctor tells me that it is ,"Just anxiety which led to a Panic attack." I was floored. He also called me a nervous nelly and prescribed me some Xanax. I finally got out of there and got home. I have to tell you that after that day I haven't felt like my old self. I knew things had changed for me.

I won't go into much more of hospital visits. I did end up there again a week later for the same reason only it was 2am. By this time I was getting pretty crazy wondering what was I going to do about this. I didn't have a clue how to proceed on how to handle all this new feeling of anxiety and daily panic attacks. I really didn't know anyone at the time who had went through all of this. At least I didn't think so.

As the story goes, I went back to my doctor and I told him what had happened. He proceeded to call me crazy. He actually said those words to me straight to my face. I told him I needed something to help me, like meds. I asked him for something that wouldn't get me addicted. He prescribed me Buspar. He asked me how I ended up two times in the hospital I told him that it was because he scared me, that is when he called me crazy. Who does that? What kind of doctor says that to a patient. He also told me to go see a shrink. I have to say I was shocked. My husband was really mad that the doctor spoke to me that way.

I get home and realized my life was never going to be the same.

I thought I would get better on my own. I had no idea it was going to take a while. I really don't have the patience I thought I had when it comes to getting better. I had no idea what this was all about. After about a couple of months I decided to try a different doctor who was the complete opposite of my nightmare doctor who started all this. I found this female doctor, one of my friends told me to try a female primary doctor, as they are more understanding and patient. I love my new doctor she is so relaxed. It's all about a having a good patient doctor. I went to see her and told her what was going on and what the other doctor did to me. She had me do blood work again. She did recommend me staying on my bp meds and lowered my dosage as it wasn't as bad as I was told by the other nightmare doctor. I also was put on a low dose cholesterol medicine. I was told by the other doctor that I was pre diabetic. This new doctor said no, I was not pre diabetic. She did keep me on Buspar which is non-addictive and is for anxiety and gave me low dose Xanax to use only when needed. My new doctor recommended me to try and find something to help me stay calm. Find a hobby to keep me busy. I am still trying new things to keep me busy.

I am going to leave this story here for now. I hope it shows you that you are not the only one going through anxiety and panic attacks. I have talked to a lot of people in my studies of this and got a few stories. I will share them with you throughout this book. I am hoping they will connect with you and help you in some way. That is my goal here is to help you!

CHAPTER 1

It Really Does Help To Talk About It!

Let me tell you that when the anxiety and panic attacks start to happen. You don't really want to talk about it. You are not sure what is going on. You really want to talk to someone but not really sure how to at this point. You don't know if you really want to run and hide or scream. Am I right? Look I know you are having a hard time and I promise you it will get better. I bet your sitting there reading this right now, saying "what is she talking about?" "How will I get through this and get better?" You can get better or even beat it, but it will take time and patience and courage.

I am hoping you have a great support system at home. Like a husband, family, friends to talk to about it. I am saying that it might be a good idea at first just to tell them you don't know what's going on, but you are going to find out. It will take a bit of time to even want to talk to anyone about your illness, or whatever makes your more comfortable to call the anxiety.

When I first started to talk about my anxiety of course it was with my husband. As he was around me the most. I am sure it still confuses him today. Even though I have talked to him, like a hundred times. I am here to tell you sometimes it takes 101 times for your spouse or whoever you confide in to try and get it. Like I have said before. If someone has never had an anxiety or panic attacks they will try and understand, but there is no way in reality that they could all together get it if they have never had anxiety.

I want to say that I do pray a lot, it comforts me in these troubled times. Now if you choose to, you can always pray or meditate to the one that you do believe in. You can meditate on it or journal. The only thing with journaling I found is. When you start to journal while in the midst of this life changing event at the beginning. You will find it hard to concentrate. I am not telling you not to. Surely you can try. You might be able to. I know I couldn't concentrate on anything for months when I first started getting attacks. I would try and focus and poof the thought would be gone. You could always join a group on social media until you feel comfortable going to a group out in the real outside world.

When I finally could get out of my house. I went to the gym. I had been house bound for a bit due to the anxiety and panic attacks. I went into the gym and of course my buddy who owns it gave me a big hug. Now, I don't really want to be touched at this point in my recovery. It is strange because I've always been a big hugger. She proceeded to ask me how I'm doing, where I've been. I just smiled and said, "I have had some issues lately." Now I do want to tell you that I've always been a big talker. I just told her the truth. I proceeded to tell her what had happened. All the panic attacks and anxiety and the hospital. I of course didn't go into all the little details. I really didn't even think about why I was telling her. I just blurted it all out. To my surprise she told me that she had a bad panic attack while driving one day. She told me that she was driving on the interstate to go visit her daughter which lives five hours away. She was alone traveling. Which she always loved to take off by herself. She does have a man, but she just liked to go visiting by herself sometimes. She said she was driving, then all of a sudden she had a weird feeling. Like full panic. She pulled off the road and thought she was having a heart attack. I asked her what did she do then. She proceeded to tell me that she just sat there for like ten minutes and then it passed. She got back on the road and it never happened again.

I am here to tell you that it is a shocker to me that she only had one episode. I know what you're thinking, you're thinking how in the world can she only have one bad episode and no more. I really don't have the answer for that as I am not a doctor. Yes, there are some people that only have one episode and that's it. Just as I have met other people who are on all kinds of meds and other coping mechanisms who have suffered hard for a lot of years or as few as just weeks. As I have learned that when talking about your situation with others. You will really be surprised how they open up. Some will open all the way to you and others will tell you bits and pieces. You will be surprised as to their stories. The one thing that I can take away from her story is that everyone is different. There is not one person who has the same exact symptoms as the other. I do think we all start off having the same symptoms. Then as anxiety progresses it magnifies to much different in some cases.

I found myself talking to just about anyone who would listen. It just would come out of me. I found this out by just mentioning my anxiety. Now I'm not talking about just blurting it out like some crazy person. I don't stand in the middle of the room and shout out that I have anxiety or anything like that. I am talking about like for instance. Getting my nails done or hair done. You know how you sit there and think of something to talk about. The subject would just come up. I found it very interesting that the other person would say that they had experienced anxiety too or have it. You can have the conversation with anyone. Just talk about what feels comfortable or just listen to their story.

What I would tell you is to try your best to talk to people, don't be ashamed, or embarrassed. It might take a bit of time, but I am sure you will get there. If your shy that's ok. It will come. Trust me that you are not alone in this. Keep your courage!!

LET'S TALK ABOUT IT!!

CHAPTER 2

Stories!!

Here are a few stories I thought I would share with you. These stories are of other people I have encountered along the way. You might see some similarities in them and I hope this helps you. YOU Are not alone in this. I'm hoping that they will help and encourage you to seek some way to cope with your anxiety and panic attacks.

I had to go the doctor to get BOTOX for my headaches. I have been going there for a while. I was checking out after my injections and I was waiting at the front desk. There was a young girl. I would say about 23. She was very sweet, cute, smart. You would never know just by looking at her that she had any kind of problem. I mean from the outside you would never know that she had extreme, I mean very extreme anxiety.

I started talking to her and I noticed she was a little shaky. She was the only one there for a few minutes. I asked her what was wrong. Do you remember I told you I can talk to anyone? IT'S a gift. lol. She looked at me and got all teary eyed. I asked her again what was wrong with her? I will call her LISA. She didn't want me to use her real name in my book. Lisa told me that she was feeling a little anxious. I asked her why. She told me that it was that she has had anxiety and panic attacks for four years. Now remember I told you she is only 23. Lisa told me that she also works in a night club on the weekends.

I asked her how in the world can she work in a night club with her anxiety. Lisa told me it was all about the meds. Along time ago as she calls it. Almost four years, which that is a long time to carry extreme anxiety. She was put on meds for her anxiety. Lisa told me that they were not working anymore. She didn't know how much longer she could take the loud noise at the night club. When she would be standing waiting for her drink orders, the loud music would start to make her shake and her heart pound. Lisa had all the feelings from anxiety.

When she got done with that short story. I tried to give her some advice. I introduced her to the breathing technique. Which I will go into it later in the book. Then I introduced her to some other types of medicine, more earthy and better for her to try.

We didn't know each other at all since she was pretty new there. I think I helped her a lot. Lisa, seemed more happy and confident that she might actually find some relief so she can still work both her jobs. Without the horrible effects of anxiety.

I did see her again a few months later. I asked her how she is doing. She told me she is much, much better and thanked me for my help and advice. I am very happy my little bit of advice was able to help her. She is way too young and healthy for this life changing event to totally ruin her life. I'm am glad we talked about it.

Here is another short story, but powerful. I went to see my Chiropractor. I was having so much tension in my neck from my anxiety that I had to get my neck adjusted at least twice a week. Yes, anxiety will mess with your physical being if you let it get away with it.

We were sitting there, and we were talking a bit. You know how it is. You tell the doctor about all your aches and pains. Then he tries to figure out what is wrong with you. I was telling him about my anxiety. Believe it or not, he immediately started to tell me about his anxiety and a time with a panic attack. I believe he's about 38 maybe.

Sam was doing some work in the yard. Now Sam looks to be in good health, works out. Takes care of himself.

Sam said he was working hard, and he was alone. His family was away visiting relatives. Sam, all of a sudden was not feeling so good. He went up to the house when he started feeling his heart pumping hard. Sam grabbed his chest! He said he thought he was having a heart attack. He lived way out, far from any hospital. His vision blurred, feeling numb. The whole panic attack symptoms, yet sometimes has the same symptoms of a heart attack. At the time he didn't know he was having a panic attack. He never experienced anything like it. I know it's not funny, but it was the way he told it.

He went inside the house and then he laid on the floor. While he was laying there, he thought he was having a heart attack. So, he crawled outside because he thought he was dying and didn't want to make a stinky mess in the house. He didn't want his family to come home and have to deal with that. Sam said, "I just was going to lay here and die, because there is nothing else I can do." Sam just laid there for a bit. He said after a little while he noticed he was still alive. Sam didn't say if he went to the doctor for a checkup or not. He did say that later he figured out it was a panic attack. Sam told me that he had a little anxiety once in a while, but he never experienced a bad panic attack like that before.

I had to go back to see my chiropractor again and he had yet another story for me. Here it is!

Sam told me that he had another bad panic attack two month's prior to me seeing him again. As I talked to him, the more he confided in me that he had been dealing with anxiety for a long time, maybe fifteen years. It started right out of college.

The way he told me his story was hilarious, who knew he was so funny. The anxiety and panic was not so funny. He did say he had to laugh at it now. He was fully animated telling it to me.

Sam had just got done eating his breakfast and with it he had a couple of cups of coffee. He said he was hooking up his trailer to his truck hitch and said it was pretty hot. It was July here in Florida. It was like 90 degrees plus the sun here is really hot when you're working outside, it just beats down on you. So, he starts to get a little overheated, sweaty, but of course he still keeps doing what he's doing. He then begins to get the heart palpitations again. Just like he had two months ago. He starts to think he is having a heart attack this time for sure. He grabs his chest and starts breathing hard. He gets into his vehicle and starts to drive. I don't think I would recommend this at this point. He knows the hospital is only one mile away this time. He is driving in a panic state. He calls his brother who doesn't answer. Now he doesn't pull over, which I would of suggested. He tries to make it to the hospital.

Sam finally makes it to the hospital. As soon as he sees the er sign of the hospital he starts to calm down. He gets to the hospital parking lot and sits in his car in front of the er. He just sits there for the moment. He knows now that if he does have a heart attack that someone will see him and that he can get help right away. Now what is funny about this, is that he said as soon as he realized this. His panic went away, the heart thumping went away. When he was calming down his mind went from survival mode to his reality mode. He thought to himself once again. I didn't have a heart attack, I am fine! Sam told me that he didn't want to spend a lot of money going to the er for a panic attack. So, after sitting in his car just a little bit longer, he left and went on his way.

Sam did go to a doctor the next day or so and have an ekg done. The doctor said his heart was fine and that he had a panic attack due to high anxiety.

You see his anxiety ramped him up so bad that it gave him a panic attack. He is still a very competent chiropractor. One of the best around. This taught me that even if you have anxiety or a panic attack. You can learn to keep yourself calm most of the time and push through it and do your job. If he didn't tell me about his anxiety. I would've never known it. You couldn't tell just by looking at him or talking to him that anything was wrong. I am happy I got the opportunity to talk with him, it gave me a new insight to the world of anxiety.

The last thing I want to say. Is that you are not alone in this. There are a lot of people of all professions and cultures who suffer from this life changing event.

You can and you will recover and live a great life like you are supposed to!

KEEP YOUR HOPE, DON'T GIVE UP!!

CHAPTER 3

Try to Explain to Family and Friends Why You Are Anxious!!

This is a tough one, because no one really gets it until they have experienced it themselves. I know that when I first had one it scared the crap out of me. I remember looking over at my husband's face. He looked so scared and confused. Anxiety and panic attacks are very scary, very disturbing to your mind and body. I believe if your reading my book then your have already had either an anxiety or panic attack. Am I right? I thought so. It's a rough life when you have to start dealing with all of this. You know, all the heart palpitations, vision blurred, numbness in pretty much all your body parts. Just basically you feel as if you're going die for sure.

I want you to hold on. Hold on to your life. It will get better. You have to put the work in, just don't lay there feeling sorry for yourself. Get up and fight for yourself. I'm rooting for you. I am doing my best to help you here. So please read on.

I remember when I first started getting these panic attacks. My husband would tell me to just get over it. Of course, neither one of us new at the time that it wasn't going to be that easy. No way, no how. My friends would call me and ask me where I was and why was I in hiding. I told them what was going on. I have to say the majority of my friends and family had no clue. There might have been one or two that had experienced anxiety. I think they just didn't want to tell me that they had panic attacks for whatever reason I'm not sure. Maybe they were embarrassed themselves. Or maybe they weren't sure that's what they had. Who knows.

This is why I wrote this book, because no one ever wants to just talk about it. I mean come on. We are all human. Aren't we? We must have compassion for our fellow humans. I love when you finally tell someone and they say and I quote, "Why can't you just get over it?" "It's nothing, just stop thinking about it." I really like this one. "Snap out of it." Yea that was my favorite. I am so sure that you have tried to snap out of it or all of the above. I have a question: were you able to do any of that? Nope me either.

Have you ever done this. When you're having a bad panic attack, you cover your face so the no one can see you? I have one did often. I am thinking because I am so embarrassed that I need to cover my face. I am embarrassed because I can't just snap out of it. I wish I could. Later on I found it's a really long process to get even through it. Wouldn't you agree? I also have learned is for me not to be embarrassed. I realized that there is absolutely nothing to be embarrassed for. I mean come on. We didn't wish this on ourselves. We are tying our best to understand it ourselves.

When I first started with these panic attacks and severe anxiety. I didn't even try to explain to anyone. I mean how could I.

Did you try? I don't think so. The reason for this is that I really had no clue what the hell was going on myself so how am I supposed to try to explain to someone else. I knew I had to try or it would only get worse with me and them.

Here I am trying to explain first to my husband. I am so sure that he didn't get it at all. Just by the look on his face. You know that look when someone gives you a look like your nuts. Yep, that's the look. You see when you're in the beginning of all this anxiety. Your mind is so foggy. You can hardly think straight. Forget about trying to concentrate on one thing. You are just trying to survive here. The one thing is for sure that you know you have to try and make someone who never had anxiety or panic attack in their life. You want them to understand what is going on with you, so here goes one idea I tried.

I am talking to my husband, he sees most of what is going on. I thought I would try him first. This is how I explained it to him.

"It is like when your standing on a curb and then you step off the curb accidentally, not looking into traffic. BOOM!! A car comes so close to you that you thought you got hit by a car but you didn't. It scared you so bad, you jumped back and it scared you so bad that your heart was pounding through your chest. You were shaking, your legs are wabbly. You thought you were going to have a heart attack. You might even have to sit down so you can that you could try and calm down. It took you several minutes before you could gain some kind of control." To start and feel better.

When I explained this scenario to him. His expression on his face was priceless. He told me that if that was what it was like to have a panic attack, that he would never, ever tell me to. "Just get over it" again. I think finally he got it. He hasn't said those words to me since. I do believe that now he is more understanding. It took a while, but I think he gets it as much as possible.

You see, you have to go to extreme things to get it across to the ones you love. Those who have never had a panic attack or doesn't have anxiety for them to see how if might feel. This does give them some sort of idea of what is going on with you.

I am sure you could think of other things that are really scary that you or them have been through that made them break down for a moment from fear. yes fear!! Did you know that FEAR is the main reason for all the anxiety and panic attacks that your are suffering from. I didn't believe this either, but since I started to study this all this mess. I have uncovered that this is the main reason for anxiety and then of course the dreaded panic attack.

Now we are going try and explain our anxiety. I thought long and hard on this one and this is what I came up with. Here is a couple of examples.

This is a good one to explain to someone who's never been through it. You are sitting watching tv, and all of a sudden your vision starts to blur. Your legs are starting to hurt. You start feeling your arms and legs going numb, maybe your hands and feet are going numb. This scares you and you feel like there is mice running through your veins. You get a headache maybe. Now before you really go into a full blown panic attack. You know it's going come if you don't stop it now. You sure don't want another episode when your trying to relax. You start your deep breathing technique. You might even get up to walk around, that's ok.

You could tell your loved one. That if you don't get up and try to walk off the anxiety that you will have a full blown panic attack and that you really don't want to do that. Trust me, they will either leave you alone or try and help you. Just explain that you don't need there help at that moment. I find that this is because you don't want anyone to touch you, because your nerves are so jumpy. It feels like they are going jump out of your skin. You need to move around. Touch at least five things. I find this helps to redirect your brain to different thinking. Also, you might get a cold sip of water and do your deep breathing exercises.

Tell them that it's like when you're getting ready to go somewhere or do something that makes you a little nervous. Like going to a job interview or standing up doing a lecture in front of people. That nauseous feeling in the pit of your stomach. That you're a little shaky. Tell them that is the feeling of anxiety. Now they might just get that.

You could tell them about maybe use the example of them going to the dentist. Everyone is nervous about going to the dentist, some more than others. You know they can relate to this.

These are just ideas I have found to try to relate anxiety feelings to someone else who has never had anxiety. I am pretty sure they will get it after those senarios. Even if they don't understand then. At least you tried and don't be hurt by them, just move on. One day they will experience anxiety or a panic attack then they will get it. They might even come to you to tell you they get it.

You and your loved ones just have to be patient. If they love you,they will give you time to recover. Maybe they will help if you get through this if they can. Let them help you!

BE STRONG, DON'T GIVE UP!!

CHAPTER 4

Crazy Thoughts?
Are You Losing Your Mind?

Do you think you are losing your mind? Are you feeling that things are not real? That your reality is a bit skewed? Do you feel like you are going bat shit crazy? You know what they say! Where the mind goes, the body follows. Well, let's hope not!

I am here to help you with this as much as I can. Like I said, I am not a doctor by no means. I don't even try to act like one. You are getting a real person's point of view and experiences. Not just mine, I have gotten stories from people who all say the same thing. "I feel like I'm losing my mind!!"

You are not, I repeat. You are not losing your mind! You do have to learn how to control your thoughts for sure. That's the one thing about anxiety that is probably the thoughest. Controlling your mind, keeping those nasty negative, crazy thoughts in check. Trust me, they will run and ruin your life if you let them!

Here is my version of thinking I was losing my mind. I have learned and still learning how to keep my mind in check with reality.

It started with my very first panic attack. I was walking through my house and all of a sudden I got real bad tunnel vision. It felt like the floor was moving. I had to sit down and pray that it wasn't. I sat there for a little while. Trying to tell myself, that there is nothing wrong with me. Yes, its ok to talk to yourself, just don't answer back. lol. I sat there and got my mind straight finally for the moment anyway. I say the moment because I started having a lot of moments like that for maybe six months. I have to say that when you first start this anxiety roller coaster. All kinds of things happen to your mind and your body. If you have had these weird moments of un-reality, then you know what I'm talking about. They can be very scary. This is when you start to think that you are losing your mind. I forgot to mention that right after that happened, the floor moving. I had an awful panic attack. I would say that the attack lasted a good five minutes. I know your thinking that's not long. But, if you have had a panic attack, you know that's a long time. Usually an attack will not last that long.

Here's another weird, crazy thought. I think this one you can relate to. I started feeling that every day and I mean every day. Like I am talking 24/7, I thought I was going to die. Yup, just lay down and die. I think this anxiety and panic attacks is way worse than menopause. I wonder if you women who have been through menopause can relate? If you are a man, then you know it's a rough road. Of course, it's all in your mind, not reality. It takes a long time to get through these weird feelings. If you don't watch it, you might just lose your mind. You have to find a way to control those crazy thoughts.

I know that your thinking! How am I supposed to do this? You can do it. Now if you get really, I mean really irrational thoughts, then you might just want to go see a professional. I mean a psychiatrists or therapist. Someone who can help you, someone to talk to in private. I got real lucky that I pulled myself out of most of those crazy awful, life draining thoughts. Those crazy thoughts are not completely gone, I get them from time to time when my anxiety is high. I have to remind myself that they are not real.

I really think it helps if you have someone you can confide in. Even better if they have had or are still going through the same thing. I have a friend who I would call anytime day or night. She had been going through the anxiety and panic attacks episodes for fifteen years. Thank God, she knew how to calm me down. Actually, she is the one who told me about the deep breathing technique. It really does help. I will tell you about it soon. If by some chance you don't have that help. I encourage you to learn this technique. I also would encourage you to maybe talk to your primary doctor about getting some meds to help you through all of this. I would suggest finding a good one, with lots of patience and knowledge would help on the subject. No, not all doctors are the same. Of course, you probably already know this. I would get on some meds that are non-addictive for sure. There are some that are available.

Here is another thought and tool I found useful. You do not have to ride these panic attacks out. Riding it out means, to just let if finish. You might think, like riding out a cold or something. Well, I am here to tell you that there is a better way to stop it. Even before it gets started. I will go into this later in the book.

The other bothersome crazy thought is always thinking your going to die. The reason I found this is because of all the symptoms of anxiety and panic attacks. Like the rapid heart beating, the blurred vision, the numbness in your face, arms, legs, hands , feet. Bad headaches, upset stomach, sometimes chest pain and your throat feeling like it's going to close up on you. Some of these symptoms are a lot like a heart attack or stroke. Now I am not telling you to ignore them at first, but after a few trips to the hospital and a lot of doctor visits and checkups. You finally figure out that it's just your anxiety, heading towards a panic attack. You have to train your mind and body, that it's just your anxiety, don't panic. Do self-talk, it comes in real handy in these times. I am sure you don't want to make daily trips to the hospital. It is costly and just will make you worse. It also just drains you soul!

You are not going to die or have a heart attack from a panic attack! Keep telling yourself that. I know it feels like it. But, if you can tell yourself that every time you start to feel bad, it just might help stop the panic before it gets bad. Your welcome, "smiley face."

Remember, self- talk. Tell yourself when the anxiety is ramping up. That you are fine, you're not having a heart attack or stroke. I know brain fog kicks in when having anxiety. It is all part of the anxiety roller coaster. You have to stop it with self- talk and breathing technique before it goes into a panic attack. You can do this. It just takes practice and patience.

When a bad thought enters your mind, just put a positive thought to replace it. Tell yourself that these crazy thoughts are not real. They will pass in a few minutes. Don't be embarrassed. You can self -talk anywhere, even in public. You can do the deep breathing exercises too. They will help a lot.

Also, I found out that the heart pumping in my chest is do to all the adrenaline that was going through my body. Believe it or not that helped me a lot with my anxiety. You just have to accept what is going on in your life right now. Accept your anxiety and learn to live with it. Learn to manage your panic attacks and one day they won't be so bad, they might even go away. Stay calm and think positive thoughts as much as you can to get through the rough times. I know it will be hard at first, but after a time you can learn to live again. Most of all. Don't worry about what others think of you. It is your life, your battle. You will win!

YOU ARE NOT CRAZY!!!

CHAPTER 5

Fear...Let's Talk About It... Let's Deal With It!!

Do not let Fear steal your joy in life! Anxiety is no more than severe sensitivity, kept alive by confusion and fear.

Fear can come from a shock to our nervous system, such as an overwhelming surgical operation, or a death of a loved one. Or it can come from some kind of confinement or accident. It also could come from bad news, a family member or a friend that is dying.

Fear could come from all sorts of things. Fear can show its ugly head anytime it feels like it. I talk about fear as if is its own thing. I really do believe that it is. Fear is always around, but I think you can get a handle on it. I mean you can develop fear just from small events, or for no reason at all. I don't even think even the smartest doctors can describe it or tell you how not to fear.

I can only give you some suggestions as how to handle or manage it. I don't believe in the face your fear thing. Because some fear should not be faced. Some are legitimate, like fear of dying. I think a lot of people suffer from this fear. Or if you do some things like jumping out of a perfectly good airplane, sky diving. You don't have to do that to make your fear of heights go away. I am thinking that it will not take away your fear of heights. It just might make you have a fear of airplanes. lol. Which if you do stupid stuff, as in dangerous stuff. Then that is just plain stupid. I know that we agree on this. Here is a real fear. Like being afraid of lightning storms. I live in Florida. Now Florida is known as the capital of the USA for its most lightning strikes of anywhere else. I mean the sky to ground lightning thing. I believe I have always had this fear. As soon as my anxiety started. It is a struggle to not flip out when storms come through. Now I believe this is a for real fear. I am fearful of lightning hitting my tree or my house. Yes, it does happen here. I mean you hear stories of people getting hit by lightning on the beach a lot down here. I love the beach, but I know when I hear thunder to get off the beach. So yes, this is an absolute real fear.

You can be a little bit afraid of something in your past that never really bothered you too much. But when you get this anxiety it can make that little bit of fear get extremely big. Let's say in your life you are a little bit scared of snakes, or reptiles of any kind. Then one day you go outside and there is a black harmless snake right outside your door and you almost step on it. Now I have been through this a lot. So, I watch my step. Now I don't live in the woods. It happens a lot in the hot weather. Now since your really in a sensitive state anyway. Your fear kicks in and here comes high anxiety and if you don't stop it your panic will set it. This is what I mean by real fear. Real fear is something that can actually harm you.

I am sure you've heard the flight or fight response. That is where you feel fear and either you fight whatever is scaring you or, you flight, like in run like hell. Fear itself is the cause of gradually stimulating your adrenalin. Releasing nerves to produce disturbing sensations. These sensations are the ones we have been discussing here in my book. These sensations that a person feels is new, so it gets the adrenalin pumping throughout your whole body. When this happens and its new to you, it will scare you which will put a big fear in you. Then you become afraid of the fear itself. It seems like a never-ending road.

Now when there is no real danger, no real fear. Then I call that. Fortune telling. It is where your trying to see the future. This is usually bad thinking. Your fear has taken over your thoughts. Like the fear of dying,or getting into accidents. Things like that. Your imagining the worst scenarios. This is not real fear at all, but if you focus on it too much it will drive you mad. You have to watch your thoughts. When you start thinking these not real fear. I am telling you to stop it right in its tracks. Tell yourself that it is stupid, and it's not real at all. There is no fear. Tell yourself it's just not real. Stop thinking about it and move on. You will see just changing your mindset and pay attention to what you are thinking and immediately change what your thinking to something nicer. It will go away. Remember, practice, patience and trust in your-self.

YOUR ONLY OBSTACLE IN LIFE IS FEAR ITSELF!!

CHAPTER 6

Fear of Being Alone!!

Fear of being alone after you have ended up in the hospital two times in two weeks for severe panic attacks due to high anxiety was a very big deal for me. I was afraid of being alone in my own house. I mean come on, why in the world would I be afraid to stay in my own house by myself. Your house is supposed to be your safe place. Well, if you have suffered from anxiety and panic attacks. You really don't want to be alone at all. Except of course if you are in the middle of an attack, but that is only for a few seconds or minutes, depending on the severity of it. You don't want anyone to touch you or get near you at that moment.

When you are at home with anxiety, no matter how severe your anxiety is, it is a bit scary. You know that feeling. The feeling of what happens if I am really having a heart attack. Those crazy thoughts we discussed in the last chapter. You are playing the fortune telling game. The what if game! Do not, I repeat, do not get sucked into this thinking or you will get right back on that hamster wheel.

When you are alone in your house and you start to get anxious. You will have to do something to not panic and go to the hospital again for another doctor telling you that you are a nervous nelly and to go see a therapist. That's was what the second doctor at the hospital told me to do. lol. not funny really! So, here are some ideas that I will give you. I do these things and it keeps me out of the hospital. We all know that the hospital is the very last place we want to be with our high nervous nelly anxiety self!

The first thing I recommend is when you start thinking those bad negative thoughts to try and change them as fast as you can. Think of something positive. This might be tough at first, especially if you have brain fog. You know where you cannot focus on anything at all. With practice it gets easier. Trust me on this. When you get your thinking straight, then you start to calm down a bit.

The second thing I would do is call someone who you have been confiding in. Tell them that you're really anxious and need to talk to them for a minute or five minutes. Just enough to help you to switch your mind to reality. This person should already know what's going on with you. I will hope they will have patience with you. Now, even if they have never experienced anxiety, if you have had a talk with them, they should be able to at least listen and tell you to calm down. They should tell you that you are ok, that you are not having a heart attack. They should tell you to do your deep breathing exercise. I am telling you, this will work for you. I have talked to several people about the breathing technique and they swear by it.

Now, maybe you don't have anyone that you can call at that moment. Then you have to rely on yourself. I know it's rough to do this. I have had to do this often. You can do it! You walk around your house or sit down if it's really bad. Touch five things around you. Do your deep breathing exercises. You do not want to lay down at all, even though you really want to. Do not do it! The reason is that it will for sure raise your anxiety. The mind and body does not react well to this. I laid down a couple of times at first and trust me it did not go well. All it did was make me worse. When I laid down, I could feel my heart beating faster, and when you feel this you automatically begin to panic. So, get up and walk around the house or kitchen. While you are in the kitchen, grab some cold water, of course when you can breath better, take a sip of water or two sips of cold water, do not guzzle it down. You don't want to shock your body to much after that panic episode.

You are not going to die from a panic attack. So, stop thinking you are! You will not die from anxiety. Now they might make your life miserable, but you will not die. So just remember that and tell yourself that every time you start to panic.

I know it got better for me when I got all my tools I needed to help me to manage my anxiety and panic attacks. The tools I mean are the deep breathing exercises and meds if you need them. Which most people I have talked to do need them. They take some kind of meds to help. You also as I have said before. Do self- talk, meditate, pray.

I also think that getting out of your house every day. I mean really make yourself do it. I know it's hard, but you will sure feel better. Yes, even if you go out for a short walk, do it. The point is to take your mind off of your anxiety and yourself.

I have come to except that I will probably have this anxiety forever. I am hoping that I can control it enough with time that it won't ruin the rest of my life and I can function somewhat normal again. Do not be afraid to except that this might change your life. If you push yourself to hard and try to ignore the anxiety and panic attacks it will not help you at all. Maybe, just maybe you won't have it forever!

Look I know you are scared. I have felt it too, I still do. But, I push through that fear as much as possible, I never stop trying. Remember, fear is not real in our anxiety world. Do not be afraid of fear! You will have to face this particular fear if you want to recover at all.

YOU ARE NOT ALONE!!

CHAPTER 7

Fear of Leaving the House!!

Here is a google search of this phobia they call Agoraphobia. It says that often it develops after having one or more panic attacks. It says it can lead to various fears, such as open spaces, close spaces such as elevators. The google search says it might make it difficult for a person to leave the house. I mean you could end up house bound for sure. I have went through being house bound, do to anxiety and panic attacks for about a year. I still struggle with it sometimes.

I did tell you before, that anxiety and panic attacks come from fear. Then of course you fear having the fear. It is a never-ending cycle, that's why I call anxiety, being on the hamster wheel. Going round and round. Or the road that never ends. You might even call it the anxiety roller coaster.

Here is my version of being housebound. I like calling it housebound, sounds better. I mean do we really want to think we have yet another issue to deal with? I don't know about you, but I really don't want to deal with a named phobia! Here goes my definition of Fear of leaving the house! Are you ready?

My version of Fear of the leaving the house is much more intense, much more debilitating. I am sure you know how this feels if you have this awful feeling. It is like living in your own prison with your own anxious thoughts. It got so bad for me that I couldn't go anywhere without having a panic attack. Oh, and forget about going by myself. There was no way I could go out alone for fear of having an attack while in the car or in public. I don't think anyone has any idea how this feels unless they have went through it themselves. It makes you depressed and mad. Most of the time you have no clue how to fix yourself. I call it fixing myself because I feel like I am broken. I know that you feel the same way. I think you can relate to this.

It really does seem that the more you dwell on your anxiety and stay in the house, the worse it gets. I remember getting ready to go somewhere. I am just taking driving to the store! I would get dressed and the whole time I would be sweating, my heart beating fast. You know what

I am talking about. All those awful anxiety feelings. In the beginning of this. I couldn't make it to the car, and the car in parked in my garage. It took me along time. I am saying almost a year to be able to get out of my house in my car and drive alone more than a couple of miles without having a full blown panic attack. I mean I would go for small walks around the block. Now that took about three months. I am not putting a time limit on here. I have no clue how long it would take anyone to get out of there house. The sooner the better is the key. Baby steps, take baby steps. You have to do something, you surely don't want to be housebound for the rest of your life. That is no way to live and you really want to enjoy life. Don't you? Yes, you do!

You want to read something funny? I have always loved being at home. As a matter of fact, I have worked from home for the majority of my life. I also liked going out with friends, going to the gym, the beach. I love to have fun. So, you might think that this housebound thing I could get used to and it wouldn't bother me. Let me tell you that if you forced to stay home it's not so much fun anymore. Now is it? Hell no is my answer!

I am sure you can relate to this one! How about making excuses to yourself for not going out! You might even keep changing your appointments all the time. Thinking you will feel better and be able to get out of the house the next time. Well the next time comes and you know that you have to get out this time. Maybe it is a doctor appointment or your hair done. Or maybe the dentist. So, what do you do? You cannot keep missing all your appointments, you just can't. You know it is not good for you, mentally or physically. This is what I did for a very long time. I would ask my husband to take off work and take me. I mean drive me to my appointments. Even then I would have a panic attack every time I would go. This went on for way to long.

Then I realized one day that I could not keep bothering him to take me. I mean one day you have got to get your shit together and take care of yourself. Be independent again! I used to tell myself and still do sometimes. That what if something happened to him, I have no one else who would do this for me. I have got to get it together somehow, some way.

This is what I did to get my independence back. Yes, it is a process. I would make my appointment. The day of the appointment I would get dressed and try not to think about anything, especially my anxiety or fear. I would wait till I was all the way dressed then I would call an Uber. Kind of makes me laugh now! But let me tell you at the time it was not funny at all. So, I would call the Uber and it would show up really quick. You know they are quick to show up! Then I would run, well not run, but walk fast to the car. They already have the address I go too, so I don't have to even talk to them if I don't want to. Of course I did. I found myself not able to shut up when I went out in public. I am sure this is from staying in the house by myself for way to long. But in talking to the driver, I had one driver who told me she had anxiety and just took a Xanax when she was driving. Well that made me a bit nervous, but she proceeded to tell me it was the lowest dose possible and she only took it when her anxiety was keeping her from working. So guess what, that put me at ease. I realized that If I could get some kind of meds that weren't addicting and wouldn't impair my driving. I might just be able to get out of the house. I am not saying for you to drive impaired at all. I am just saying if you can find some meds that are mild, but help your anxiety. Then that might help you to get out of the house.

The main thing I did to get out of my house. Was I just kept telling myself that I had to. I didn't want to live like this anymore. I needed to get out and live life. I know it is hard, but I am so sure you can do it. It really is a mind thing. I know I keep telling you that ,but it is true.

To finish this up. I would just take an Uber, when you first start getting out of your house and then I would drive my car around the block. Then after a bit, I would drive to the store. I still have anxiety, I take my meds prescribed to me by my doctor and I don't think about it. I get dressed, get in my car and hit the road.

You should go outside every morning, get going! You will have some anxiety ,do your deep breathing. Even if you have a panic attack before you leave the house. It will end soon and then you can go. But, do think about taking the Uber or someone taking you to your appointments so that you don't miss them. That will make it worse for you. Take a step outside your house. I also want to say that if you are shaky when walking. That is a sign of anxiety, get a cool walking stick at first. This helps your balance and your confidence. Don't be embarrassed to help yourself. Who cares what other people think! It is your life your saving!

STAY STRONG—IT IS YOUR INDEPENDENCE!!

CHAPTER 8

Fear of Driving!!

The fear of driving is a very scary thing! You can learn how to get back to driving and your freedom! It takes a bit of time and patience. Just don't think that your life is over. After you start to manage your fear-based anxiety and panic attacks, you can get to driving by yourself again with happiness.

Here is a quick story of my experience. Then I will move on to helping you with this problem. I again want to say to you, just trust me, you can get through it.

I was driving to the gym one day, this was right after my severe panic attacks, which I had went to the hospital two times in two weeks. Thinking I was having a heart attack, which turned out to be anxiety and panic attacks. I loved the gym, I was going to the gym at least five to six days a week for years, before all of this issue came up. I had joined a gym, two months before all of this happened. It was a new gym in my area, just about ten minutes from my house.

Now I didn't really like the drive to that gym because it had an intersection that was frequently having accidents. I mean you couldn't go through the green light without someone trying to run the red light, so you had to be very cautious. I think I am a very good driver, I drive like a grandma I've been told that since I started driving way back when. I am a good defensive driver.

One day I was driving to the gym. I was real anxious anyway. Of course, it is my anxiety ramping up. I am really trying to calm down. I get over the small bridge and come to the light. Now, let me tell you. My anxiety was already through the roof, but I was going to fight through it anyway. I get up to the light and stop, waiting. The light turns green, I proceed with caution, and some idiot decides to run his red light in front of me. I am so glad I payed attention. I almost hit him.

Well, let me tell you. I hit the panic button, or my mind did and then of course my body went right along with it. I passed through that light safely. I say its about two minutes after the light to the gym, which is no big deal, usually. As soon as I got through the light, I was getting a full-blown panic attack. At this time in my journey I had not learned any tools to help me to stop it before it got so bad. I realized at that moment that I didn't have any turn off. You know, where you can get off the road safely. There were no side streets to pull off on. I had to drive those awful two minutes to the gym.

Now I know what your thinking. Your thinking well, two minutes isn't that bad! Let me tell you, and if you ever have been through a severe panic episode. That those two minutes seem like forever. I get to the gym and I am sitting in my car having a very bad attack. I mean I could not breath, at least I thought that. Which was not true or I wouldn't be sitting here writing to you. I sit there for another, who knows how long. I am thinking like maybe fifteen minutes. I finally start to calm down. Now at this point I should of just went back home, but the fear of driving through that light again was scaring the crap out of me.

I went into the gym. My legs were shaking so bad from fear that I could barely walk. Yes, sometimes fear based anxiety can make your body parts hurt. Mine just happened to be my legs. Weird, I know. I get to the dressing room and have yet another panic attack. This one was not as bad, yet it was bad enough for a couple of women to ask me if

I am ok. I told them I just was having a anxiety moment. One of them told me that she too has this issue of anxiety. I told them I was fine, then I proceeded to push through and go on the elliptical.

An elliptical machine is one of my favorites. Gives you a great workout and is not as dangerous as a treadmill. I was doing like forty minutes a day on this thing. I get up on it this particular day and all of a sudden another panic attack starts. I am like, what the hell is going on here. Why am I having so many of these. I literally pushed myself to do at least twenty minutes in the panic state. This was rough, I do not recommend this to anyone. I was determined to exercise this out of me. I am laughing about it now, but it was not funny at all then. I mean I really did think I could tough it out. I get off this machine and decide to call it quits for the day.

I did make it home without another episode. Right then I decided to get a hold of this. I can say I didn't go back to that gym after that. I was done with that. It did help me to understand that I had to stop these panic attacks before they start. They are very debilitating. If you have been through one, you know its awful. So my suggestion is to get ahold of your anxiety before it even starts to stick its ugly head out and give you a panic attack. You have to be determined and have courage and confidence in yourself.

This event changed my life for sure. After that I could not drive for along time. Remember I told you I had to catch rides or go in a uber? This went on for almost a year. I have two vehicles and could not drive any one of them. Then when I did drive by myself I had to have someone with me. The fear of driving alone had set in. I was afraid to drive alone, the feeling of what if I pass out or lose my vision while driving. You know that one of the effects of panic attacks for me is a feeling of passing out or losing my vision, not completely blind but very blurry vision. In my mind it was telling me that I could pass out or not see clearly and kill me and someone else. You will not do any of these things. Fear based anxiety is a liar, not real. But it can screw you up in all kinds of ways.

This stupid fear crippled me from going to work or my favorite places, the gym, the beach, shopping, nails, hair, and doctor appointments. All of the things that life is made up of. Through this all I started of course losing my confidence of driving. Well really confidence of everything. I think that is the main thing that happens when you start getting anxiety. You lose your confidence. I will get into regaining your self-confidence soon.

I do have some help here on how to get back to driving. Like I have said several times in my book. I am not a doctor. I am telling you all these things from my personal and other people experiences. I also had done a lot of research on the subject. I mean a lot. I wanted to get better. I went to several doctors who could not help me at all. The only thing they ever want to do is put me on meds. They have no clue as how to help you manage your own anxiety. Oh, they might tell you to do yoga or something like that. I am telling you that you can do downward dog or whatever it's called. But it will not help you train your mind to manage your anxiety or stop your attacks.

I believe I have found the way to stop your panic attacks before they get a hold of you. Now managing your anxiety is a whole different thing. Let's get started on how I managed and investigated how to get back to driving with confidence and by yourself. Yes, I said by yourself. All alone and enjoying driving again. Enjoying your freedom again.

Tips and tools on how to get back to your driving:

STEP 1: GO SIT IN YOUR CAR EVERY DAY, DON'T EVEN GIVE IT A SECOND THOUGHT.

Just go get in your car and just sit there. Yup, just sit there. Relax, look around. If your sitting in your garage. Do not turn your car on. Just sit there and feel your seat. Feel how comfortable it is. Put your hands on the steering wheel. Remember how good it felt to drive to where ever you wanted to go. You just got out and went. Think about that positive experience.

Do this everyday for at least five minutes. There is no set time of day here, do it whenever you want to. Just make sure it's every day. No excuses. Tell yourself that you are fine, everything is great. You are going to get better. Tell yourself that you love to drive and you believe that you are a good, safe driver. You don't want to be stuck in your house forever. You want to get out and go places and see people. Yes, you do!!

This my friends is called facing your fear. It's a way to get started on your recovery of driving.

STEP 2: SET UP A NEW GOAL EVERY DAY.

If you are in your own driveway, then get in your car like you have been practicing and start the car. Now make sure if you have a garage that you open the garage door and pull out onto the driveway. Yes, I have to tell you that because your mind of anxiety might not tell you that. You're out in your driveway. All you have to do is go in reverse, then stop and go into drive. At this point your still in your driveway. You can do it a couple of times. Then stop and look around, you can even roll your window down. Look around, smell the air. Sit there for a moment or two then pull back into your garage or just put the car in park in the driveway and turn the car off.

There you have done the hardest thing yet. I am very proud of you. It's the beginning of your getting back to driving. Have a coke and a smile!!

STEP 3: TAKE A DRIVE AROUND THE BLOCK!!

Yes, I said take a drive around the block. Get in your car and take a drive around your block. If you feel ok, then go around the block again. I know this sounds boring, but it works. I would say do this every day. Do it as much as you can. I say with in a week you will feel good about driving. You might even want to go further.

STEP 4: WHILE DRIVING TURN ON YOUR MUSIC.

Maybe you have some cd's or a music list you listen too. Turn it on. You can turn it on low at first. I do recommend that so you can pay attention to the road. When you feel more confident in your driving again, then you can turn it up. When you get into driving again. You can sing along with the music. This is a great stress reliever. Who cares if you can't carry a tune. Sing along anyway!

STEP 5: TAKE A DRIVE TO THE GROCERY STORE.

Now if you want to, take someone with you at first. After while, I cannot tell you exactly how long. It just depends on the person. You will eventually be able to go to the store by yourself. That will be awesome. I know you can't wait.

STEP 6: DO NOT WORRY ABOUT WHAT THE OTHER DRIVERS ARE THINKING ABOUT YOU.

I am telling you that they are not thinking about you at all. They are doing there own driving. I am sure some or most of them. Are dealing with there own life issues. If for some reason someone is on your tail,or pulls out in front of you. Just keep driving, don't worry about them. You know you're a good driver. Just do your defensive driving, like you learned in school. You will be fine. Be proud of yourself. You're driving again, you are not stuck at home.

STEP 7: THINK HAPPY THOUGHTS.
Turn those negative thoughts into positive thoughts. You can do this, I am here to testify that it will work. Takes a little bit of practice. You can do it.

STEP 8: REMEMBER YOUR DEEP BREATHING ALL THE TIME.
It will refocus your mind from anxiety to reality.

STEP 9: BABY STEPS.
The one thing I wouldn't do is drive yourself with someone who makes you nervous while your driving. Make sure you take someone who is calm and helps you remain calm yourself. You don't want to take someone who is afraid of you driving, or distracts you. Take your calm friend or loved one.

STEP 10: YOU SHOULD PULL OF THE ROAD WHEN YOU START TO FEEL DIZZY, BLURRED VISION OR IF YOUR FEELING ANY HIGH ANXIETY COMING ON.

Try and do this before the panic sets in. If your driving with someone in the car, just tell them you're feeling real anxious and you have to pull off for a minute to regain your composure. They will understand. So pull over off the road in a safe place. Turn your engine off, get out of the car and walk around the car of just stand by it. Breath the air. Touch the car. Do your deep breathing exercises.

Tell yourself that you are ok. Talk to yourself, tell you, that you can drive safely. The feeling will pass soon. Then get back in your car and keep going. When you do this several times, you will eventually be able to drive without having to get out of the car. You will find out that you can float through the weird feeling and keep driving safely. I will say it again. Be patient with this. PLEASE don't get discouraged. You can do it!

YOU WILL BE DRIVING LIKE THE WIND SOON!...FREEDOM!!

CHAPTER 9

The Awful Morning Feeling!

Waking up in the morning with high anxiety is not a good way to start your day. Now I know you have done this. I think anyone of us who have suffered with this issue has woke up feeling awful. You get woke up with heart palpitations thinking of course that your having a heart attack. It is the worst. I know its exhausting. You either lay there or jump out of bed real fast. Either way it scares you. You figure out in a few minutes that you are not having a heart attack or dying.

In the beginning of anxiety and panic attacks. You don't know what is going on. You might ask yourself over, and over again. Why am I waking up to these attacks. Why are they waking me up? You might have had a great night the night before, so you don't understand this at all.

You are not alone. My belief is that you have so much anxiety in your system, that it's going to just show up whenever it feels like it. Maybe your going to sleep really anxious, but you don't realize it. I am not a doctor so I can't say either way. It just happens. Does it really matter as to why? No, it really doesn't. What matters is how to manage it, or how to think about it so it stops doing that.

Now again this will take some time and patience. I have had these morning episodes for a while. I had to tell myself to calm down. The pounding in my heart is a adrenaline pumping in me to get my anxiety going. The pounding in your chest is exactly that, adrenaline. I actually was told this by my primary doctor, who I believe. Even though she would never admit it, has anxiety. I got the idea that she is anxious, because she would tell me almost everything I had wrong with me is from my anxiety. Or it could be she treats a lot of patients with anxiety.

The only real good advice here is to not let it ruin the rest of your day. Now, I know what your thinking. How am I supposed to do that? Well, let's just say it takes time. Yes, time. One day you will just wake up and you won't get those palpitations anymore. I truly think that if you do not pay attention to them, that they will go away on there own.

It took me awhile to make them stop. I never thought they would, but they did over time. When I would get one, I would tell myself. I am not having a heart attack, it's just my adrenaline. I am fine.

Here is some more advice. When you wake up in the morning. Get out of bed. Don't lay there feeling sorry for yourself. If you have bad anxiety when you wake up. You can lay there for a few minutes. Then get up. I know it will be hard, you can do this. The reason I say to get out of bed when you first wake up in the morning. Is that you don't want to give your anxiety time to really go into a bad panic attack. Get up, go to the bathroom. Do your regular morning routine you did before all this started happening. Try not to think about how you woke up. Yes, I know its hard. You have to do this to get better.

If you have family living with you, that's even better. Something to keep you busy. If you are alone. Get up. Turn the t.v. on or go for a walk. Just don't think of how you woke up.

I was reading some book that said when these morning attacks start to happen. To change your room around, this refreshes your mind. I mean not at that moment, but later. It is like a small shock to your mind. Changes things up. Takes your mind of yourself. You can try, see if it helps you.

Just don't get discouraged or depressed when you keep waking up in this nervous state. The anxiety will ease up all the way around if you just accept it. Yes, you have to accept that you might have anxiety for along time. Just remember, even though you woke up bad. You don't have to let it ruin your day!!

GET UP AND GET GOING!!

CHAPTER 10

Sleeplessness

Here is a very important part of your life. I know all of the symptoms of anxiety and panic attacks are important to cope with. I truly believe that if you don't get your sleep in. At least seven to eight hours a day it will be very hard on your mind and body. I am sure you already know this, but I just wanted to make sure I hit on this subject. Remember I said, "where the mind goes, the body follows?" Yes, it is so very true!

I have always been a light sleeper. When anxiety started it just made it worse. I have been taking over the counter sleep aids for about two years. I started taking them because during and after menopause. I would only sleep like two hours, then wake up. Then go back to bed, then wake up two hours later. In other words, I was waking up every two hours I was exhausted. The sleep aid works wonders. I finally was sleeping all night through. I was thrilled. Then this anxiety and panic attacks started.

I am telling you my story, so that you don't feel alone. I am sure a lot of people suffer with sleeplessness. Are you suffering from not sleeping good? I bet you are. There is relief believe or not! I'm going to do my best to tell you how to get your sleep back. I mean really good sleep. So that you feel bright and sunshine the next day.

The thing is that your body will not let you go to long without sleep. It will shut you down eventually. I really don't think you want that. You don't want to fall asleep when you need to be awake. Am I right? You will be forced to sleep.

Now again, I am not a doctor, I am just telling you what worked for me and some people I know and some I interviewed for this particular chapter. I am going to believe that you will be able to sleep peacefully again, even with anxiety. Yes, it is possible.

Here is a good tip for you to remember, this helps a lot. You have to accept your anxiety for what it is. Yes, I said accept it. It is the way over the top exaggerated response of your sensitized nerves. In another way to say it is. Your nerves are highly sensitive to everything. I mean everything. You know the feeling I am sure of it.

When I first started getting this anxiety. I would lay down and as soon as I got somewhat comfortable. My chest would start acting up. You know the heart palpitations, the adrenaline I talked about before. I mean awful palpitations, I was for sure that it was the heart attack scare. It wasn't of course. It takes time to learn that it's not a heart attack.

I would lay there telling myself that I was ok, that I wasn't going to die. I would have to get up and walk around a bit, so I wouldn't go into a full panic mode. I had just had my heart checked. Nervous nelly, as I was called. I got an ekg and echocardiogram just to make sure I was ok, because of my nervous mind thinking everything was wrong with me. It all came back with good results. I had proof my heart was good for my age. I had to keep reminding myself all the time my heart is good. Yes, I would recommend at least getting your blood pressure checked by a doctor and if your nervous like me, get a ekg done. There not expensive. Well worth your inner piece of mind.

Let's talk for a moment about the pulsating heart palpitations you can feel when your laying down. Here it is. It's the main artery in your body, the aorta, it is pumping blood to your lower body and legs when you lay down. The noise you hear when you press your ear on your pillow is the blood pumping through your brain. This is a good thing, it's supposed to do this. You are just more sensitized to it when your laying down. Do not be scared of this. I found this out by doing more research, because I was tired of feeling and hearing those sounds when I was trying to go to sleep.

When you can remind yourself of this. Believe it or not ,you will start to relax. This was a huge deal for me. I mean a great breakthrough. I finally could lay there and when it would start. I would remind myself all the things I just told you. Guess what? It is not so bad now. I am telling you it's all in your mind. The anxiety roller coaster can be slowed down and maybe stop one day. Once you accept it and learn to manage it. Your sleep and your whole life will get better.

You have to calm your mind, yes it is possible. I do a lot of self-talk through out the day and especially at night. I pray a lot. You can pray or meditate before you go to sleep. Tell your mind to ease up on you and tell it to just relax. If a negative thought pops up in your head, just tell it to go away. If you keep doing this, it will go away.

I am not telling you to go on meds. I am telling you to talk to your doctor about some sleep aids. Do not be ashamed to take them. Your sleep is very important. Take them if you can. I will not tell you to count sheep. Doesn't work at all. You have to take something to help you sleep. I think we all do when we go through this from time to time. I would also maybe get a fan, it helps to block out unwanted noise that might keep you awake. Clear your mind. Everything else can wait till the next day. Turn your phone on silent. Nothing ever good happens after midnight. I mean nothing. Do not worry about what someone else says to you about taking a sleep aid or thinks of you. You have to get your good sleep.

Trust me, when you start sleeping better, your anxiety will get better. The anxiety loves you not getting your rest. Get some good rest. I would also drink some water before bed. It's good for you.

GET YOUR SLEEP ON!!

CHAPTER 11

Sexual Activity with Anxiety!!

I thought I might touch on this subject as I found it does happen. I hope this helps you. If you are experiencing having trouble having sex with your lover. What I mean by that, is having sex with anxiety or getting a full blown panic attack during sex. This might not make either one of you happy. The reason I am writing this, is this has happened to me. I can't be the only one who this happens to. Right?

When you are going through anxiety. You go through times of not wanting to be touched. Now, I don't know if this is everyone with anxiety, I have found this to be true for me. I mean you don't want anyone to touch you, especially when your in having high anxiety or having a panic attack. You just tell anyone near you to not touch you. Yes, it is awful. Hopefully you have already explained this to your loved ones, so as not to hurt there feelings. It is just your sensitized nerves we have been talking about.

So when it comes to having sex with a loved one and your heading toward a panic attack it can put a damper on the whole situation. I have had my heart about to jump out of my chest when I got excited. This happened to me a couple of times and of course I had to stop. Scared the crap out of me. Now after I started to manage my anxiety, I was able to stop the anxiety from going into a full panic mode. I had to do something about it, I didn't want my marriage to suffer. I mean who wants to get a divorce because your anxiety is so high you can't have sex. Not me. So, I figured out a way to do it without having to stop in the middle. My husband and I are much happier now. "Smiling."

Here is a few pointers how to keep your love life going. First, I worked on managing my anxiety all the time. I took my prescribed medicine like I am supposed to. I exercised, prayed, stayed busy. I did all my daily routine. After a while I was ready to try and have sex again. Now, I did explain what was going on with me to my husband before, so he did have some idea of how to handle me and help me through my anxiety.

I just kept telling myself that I was ok, everything is fine. Guess what? It worked. I just wouldn't allow myself to go to those negative, crippling thoughts during our lovin. It really worked. We are both happy again. You can't let this anxiety, panic attack journey ruin your love life.

Please don't get discouraged, have confidence in yourself. Don't over think it at all. Just relax and enjoy life pleasures.

GOOD LUCK AND GOOD LOVINS!!

Things To Do and Don't Do!!

Do not run away from your fear. Do run from fear if its real. Not just a physical reaction to your anxiety.

- Do recognize that your weird feelings are from your anxiety. Do fight them, or let them float by.

- Do face whatever life throws at you in your life when it's happening, not later.

- Do not feel sorry for yourself.

- Do not dwell on the past, live in the present.

- Do look towards you happy future without anxiety or panic attacks.

- Do not be ashamed of your anxiety or panic attacks.

- Do face and accept what's going on with you.

- Do let time pass.

- Do your breathing exercises.

- Do take your meds.

- Do get some sleep.

- Do keep your mind and body busy.

- Do be happy, stay positive.

- Do pray or meditate, do whatever helps clear your mind.

WHEN YOU DO THESE THINGS. YOU WILL RECOVER!!

CHAPTER 13

Confidence

Confidence comes from courage. To do it afraid. The courage to be positive even when negative thoughts are trying to take over your mind daily. No matter what it is. I realized I lost all my confidence about my mind and my body. Of course that started as the anxiety and panic attacks got worse. I know you can relate to this and I am hoping you can get your confidence back. The confidence to be yourself again, it will happen. Takes time, patience and believing in yourself again.

I went to the doctors for everything. I mean everything. If I got a headache or a weird ache and pain. I would go straight to the doctor. Of course nothing was wrong. It was all in my mind. The anxiety just kept me in this worried state for so long.

So one day I was talking to my friend. She has been dealing with this awful, life changing event for years. I mean like almost twenty years. She is very smart and outgoing. I was talking to her one day and she told me that I had lost all my confidence in myself. I thought this was strange as I didn't realize it. I mean it never registered to me, that I had lost my confidence in myself.

I think that if she hadn't told me that. I would of never put it together. I have always been a confident woman. I still don't think that I have all the confidence I had before. I am working on it. I am a work in progress. To get your confidence back it really takes time and I have to say you have to work at it. I never realized how much work it does take to get it back. It is just a strange idea. Isn't it? It was surprising to me that all this anxiety can take away your confidence.

I think this is the reason for a lot of other things that happens to us when we go through the anxiety and panic attacks. The driving, the getting out of the house, the relationships. Almost every part of your life suffers when you don't have confidence in yourself.

One day I decided after talking to my friend and some of my own soul searching. I realized I just had to get my confidence back. I decided that when an ache or pain popped up. Which it does right out of the blue, for no reason at all. I would say to myself, self-talk. Have I had this pain or ache before? You really have to concentrate on this. I would tell myself, yes I have had this before and I was fine, nothing wrong with me. Believe it or not it really works. The pain would just go away. Then It hit me, I found a break through.

You don't focus on the pain so much. Then guess what it goes away. You have to try it! You will be amazed as to how it helps you. The other thing is of course getting out of your own negative thoughts. Replacing them with positive thoughts.

Also, get out and get to living. Go out even if your afraid. Fear will not stick around if you keep pushing it away. It will get better as you go along.

Here's a thought to help you with your confidence. Step out and find out. Find out what you are good at. Maybe you're good at some kind of athletic thing or painting, etc. You just never know until you try. If it doesn't work out then try something else. Just keep going until you find something that builds your confidence. As I was once told by my husband. "never try, never fail." Don't quit or get discouraged. I mean who knew I would become a writer. You just never know what your really good at until you try.

Confident people do not concentrate on all there weaknesses. They don't worry about what they have no control over. Even if you don't feel confident, be confident. Think that you are. It is like a game, a mind game. Think it and you will receive it.

You can find scriptures, numerous examples and ancient teachings, and philosophical quotes on confidence in your search for help on google. Try these and see if anything helps you. I found one that called out to me. It really helped me and I want to share it with you. Whatever you believe in, you must first believe in yourself. You can do it.

Here is the scripture I found in the bible. I hope it helps you as it helped me!

PEACE AND CONFIDENCE: I have told you these things, so that in Me you may have (perfect) peace and confidence. In the world you have tribulation and trials and distress and frustration, but be of good cheer (take courage; be confident, certain, undaunted!) For I have overcome the world. (I have deprived it of power to harm you and have conquered it for you.)—JOHN 16:33

HAVE PEACE AND CONFIDENCE!!

CHAPTER 14

Therapy—Help Heal Your Anxiety and Panic Attacks!

I am not a doctor. This is some therapy I have done and other people I talked to have done, it helps to get you better with your anxiety. I believe that these will help you if you do them consistently.

- Go to the doctor when you start getting the signs of anxiety and panic attacks. Just to make sure your ok.

- Get on medication if needed approved by your physician. Non habit forming. Take them.

- Use Cannabis if legal in your state. It helps you immediately.

- Deep breathing exercises. Take a deep breath in hold it for a second, blow out slowly. Do this three times. Slow and steady. Do not do it fast. It really helps in all situations, anytime, any place!

- Self-talk. Yes talk to yourself, positive thoughts only are allowed!

- Exercise. It will make you feel better, mentally and physically. It's good for your heart!

- Eat right, drink lots of water. A gallon a day is very doable.

- Get up and drive or walk somewhere daily. Even if it's around the block.

- Talk to family and friends. Find a good support system.

- If it gets really bad, go see a counselor.

Grounding—How to prevent panic attacks. This is where you do steps to get your mind to think straight. Mindful thinking it's called. You do this before you get a full blown panic attack, when you start to feeling like an attack is coming on. Breathe deeply in through your nose and out through your mouth. Do this at least three times. Remember to do it slowly. Do not do it quick or you will hyperventilate which means fast breathing. You don't want that. You want slow and deep breathing for this to help you. Here is the steps to follow. It's called the 5-4-3-2-1. Five is see, look and see five things around you. Four is touch, try to focus on touching four things around you. Three is hearing, hear three things around you. Number two is smell two different things around you that you like. And at last but not least is number one. Try and eat something, even something small, taste it. I use gum for this. You can use whatever you like, just make sure it's a small piece. Now of course don't try and eat something when your trying to catch your breath. I want to add in maybe a cold sip of water. Now this is before your go into a full blown attack. This will help stop it!

STICK WITH THIS AND YOU WILL GET BETTER SOON!!

CHAPTER 15

How to Control Your Anxiety at Work!

Here is some helpful hints that helped me and others that I talked to in the workplace!

Try and limit your in take of coffee in the morning and throughout the day. This will keep you from getting to jittery. I think coffee makes your adrenaline pump faster which makes your anxiety high.

Drink lots of water! I know what your thinking! Your thinking that you will go to the bathroom a lot. Yes, you might have to take an extra bathroom break. It does help with anxiety to get up and walk around anyway. I know that after awhile your body will get used to the water intake and you won't go as much.

Take as many breaks as possible. Just don't get into trouble. Take a short break and walk around the office whenever you can. If you can take a walk around the office outside, even better if weather permits. The idea is to get up and get some circulation going.

You might want to ask for help. If your feeling overwhelmed while working. I mean your anxiety is starting to get ramped up. You might want to delegate tasks to others. This will help lower your stress and anxiety.

Remember to do your deep breathing exercises. Yes, you can do this even in public. After some practice you can learn to do it quietly so no one will even notice. Even if they do, don't worry about it. You got to take care of yourself.

TAKE CARE AND BELIEVE IN YOURSELF!!

CHAPTER 16

Final Thought!

I just want to say thank you for reading my book! It was a rough road to write as I am still fighting the battle of anxiety myself. I have to say that after I got into writing this book, that it was well worth it. I just felt like I had to share my thoughts and experiences with you. My vision is to help as many people as I can. I am blessing each and everyone of you! I am hoping and praying that we all can get a hold of this anxiety roller coaster and be happy once again. I want us to lead a very productive, fun, loving, happy life! The one that we are supposed to enjoy, not to suffer in. I truly believe if you stick with me and do what I suggested in my book, that you can find a great way to manage this journey in your life. I promise you that if you stay strong and have confidence in yourself that you will get better and feel normal again. Thanks again!!

PEACE AND LOVE TO YOU ALL!!

www.ingramcontent.com/pod-product-compliance
Lightning Source LLC
Chambersburg PA
CBHW051000050726
47592CB00007B/2652